strong heart song
lines from a revolutionary text

poetry by

lance henson

west end press

Some of these poems were previously published in the following collections:

An Ear to the Ground, 1989 (anthology); *A Motion of Sudden Aloneness,* 1991 (chapbook); *World Literature Today,* Spring 1992 (periodical); *Returning the Gift,* 1993 (anthology).

This project is supported in part by a grant from the National Endowment for the Arts, a federal agency.

First edition, September 1997
ISBN 0-931122-86-4

Front cover illustration by Jaune Quick-To-See Smith
Cover design and book design by Michael Reed
Typography by Prototype, Albuquerque, NM

Distributed by the University of New Mexico Press

West End Press • P.O. Box 27334 • Albuquerque, NM 87125

strong heart song
cheyenne '92

nadots do mi uts e mghon baeh ni tseheskotseo
ehmin

i will walk on the ashes of the earth
singing

contents

strong heart song

untitled

it is snowing tonight
on the barren plains at wounded knee
on the hogans at big mountain
on the barricades at cornwall island
on the red earth of geronimos grave in oklahoma
it is snowing tonight
on the burnt out buildings at oka

tonight it is snowing
in the dreams of children in salvador and nicaragua
and san carlos
in the dreams of mothers in brazil and chile
and pine ridge and wind river
tonight it is snowing

the snow is ancient
within the keening wind of winter there is a prayer

si vi wo ho oh shi win
si vi wo ho oh shi win

we will not be thrown away

december 28 1990

from a journal entry 9/18/86

"the ideas of a poet should be noble and simple"
                    tu fu
                    japanese poet, 6th century

fingerprints on the window
a door knob of glass

a simple turn of wind and the earth
rearranges itself

i split cedar wood and stand for a
moment resting
surrounded by the scent of cedar
and cold

how far have we come from ourselves
that we have forgotten tu fus simple thought

the childs wide eyed stare

the moons thin arc

in early august

on a cloudy day
fields of mist on the horizon
a hint of rain strong in the air

alone for hours in the kitchen
i remember three turkey buzzards hunting just after dawn
and the way ones lungs fill with the unaccustomed heaviness
of early autumn

on a cloudy day
i taste the metal taste of aloneness

the moon somewhere mocks these words
i have no place to go

two poems from riva trigosa italy

1
just after dawn we move as in a mirror
careful not to step out

careful to silently acknowledge the dim light
from which we have come

we nod toward one another
speaking in dreaming tones
of half words

2
on a winter morning
the sky brings its light upon the orange
and yellow houses of riva

morning sounds are motorcars and in
the kitchen the sounds of women laughing

a cold dove walks on the tiled roof
across the strada

the balcony is a small garden
of chilled flowers

12/30/88

near merfert

all the way past this small creek
that flows toward the moesel river
the green fields are covered in dew

the cattle and sheep move slowly
this morning

a light rain mists over the window
i pull back the curtain and touch
the cold glass

my son disappears into the barn
i watch for a long time the darkness
he entered

and reach to light a cigar

1/4/89–2/18/92

a vermont memory

1
i follow the tracks of a snowshoe rabbit
from the place where it nestled just outside
the window
i close my eyes slowly
watch the dark trees where its tracks
disappear

2
the landscape is elegant yet dim

the mountains and unlit houses
in the distance
are a blue haze

i listen to the wind song through the window
counting us again . . .

12/25/88

riding at dusk in vermont

1
sunlight touches the treetops just outside
stannard
though the sun is fading
its light is steady and good

2
a black feather dreams about its birth
on a cedar bough just ahead

it is growing dark
the road behind me turns into
a cold scar

untitled

a man turns from glinting sunlight
and all day alone
sings into himself

we are too distant from what we have
known
the light of a thousand moons flares in
the bones of our hands
i pause to hear other words flung
into sound
my poems come slower now

escaping down long corridors where the
shadows of discordant winters dream

your voice an insistent rhythm

of leaves

in the dark trees

8/19/89

driving toward watonga to visit my grandmother

something in the gap of wind ahead
dreams reaching back toward themselves
unraveling

a spinning reed circles on a sand hill
the moons configuration

a redtail lifts just ahead of me
near swappingback mission

i would tell you that silence is the bearer
of good things
and it is your voice that is the music
most still

2/20/86
8/17/87
10/10/89

lines written at jelles house

i touch the dark moments of three am
and all that is silent is blue

the rooms of my brothers house wrapped in the stillness
of children dreaming

against the sweating windows there are
small words whispering
like a spiderweb wrought with a thousand
petals of dew gathering moonlight
these poems wait for the right hour
usually late
far from slumber and the regrets of day

all of these days wearing us thin of dreams
but for the moments when poetry
floats down like dust upon
our shoulders

and we remember we are alive

genemuiden the netherlands
11/15/90

separations

walking under the winter sky near the harbor of genemuiden
a black swan flies low over
the water

a man in a small motorized boat makes a slow
circle just beyond the path of the ferry

lost in the lines of a repeating song
the waves of weary smiles and laughter lap
at the hour i will remember passing here

again at the edges
searching through the torn dreams and faces
that make a life

a man in wooden shoes walks behind me on the
path toward town
his footsteps fading into wind

there is the deepened solitude of a far train whistle
an open sky filled with clouds

that are gray

somewhere near kalkaska michigan

in northern michigan i have
just awakened from a dream
of clove fields and rain

outside the window a gray rabbit
leans into the wind eating a
white flower

after three months of hiding
i am suddenly caught
in a dream work

to live near the edges of things

i watch the dark inside a stand
of pines
and yearn as the deepest
hidden tree
for light . . .

8/8/90

near portville ny
in memory of michael west*

my brother is walking in shadow over a bridge
we both remember
i have followed my solitude here and wander
past him toward the dark

wherever it was that silence resided
whether in the gray shoes of the poor
or the whitening smoke that rises in winter
over the sea
when i turn it is gone

in the nights somnambulance i make a small prayer

for the stars that drown and vanish
in the shameful mists of men

*for my younger brother who died at the age of 31—a victim of
americas genocidal attitudes

wo he iv* 11/29/90

the rain lies down
beside a fallen leaf

a crow
flies overhead carrying
a bright piece of string

for the first time this day
i will speak your name

waiting the night through

for the morning
star

*morning star, michael wayne henson's cheyenne
name

from indian country . . .
oklahoma city to taos new mexico 1988

its another dawn in indian country
the mist hanging heavy on the broken down cars
someones grandmother is starting a breakfast fire
in the back yard
frybread—eggs—and coffee under a cottonwood tree
a slow dog moans turning its back from the sun

the baptist mission church is boarded up
the white preacher in a 68 ford pulls a u-haul trailer
toward some other jesus road
maybe new mexico
we plains indians have our own god
we just wait until the christians wear out
we meet in the spirit of crazy horse here the sign
above the bar in hammon reads
bo diddley on the juke box scratches out sad lyrics
a kiowa girl watches from the window the policeman
watching her from a patrol car

in santa fe under the crack of cue balls a navajo
kid with a black ponytail in a karate ghi top
squints across the smoky 22 years of his life
chicanos in a corner rolling a joint
it smells of gasoline and danger on the highway north
to taos
an old woman pulls her purse closer when i walk by
in the open market
she thinks i want to steal her life

among the bright buckles and turquoise rings
a small whirlwind winds around the side of a hippies pickup
too deep in america to feel comfortable
i watch my startled face in his window
and turn away

lines from a revolutionary text I

from this train window
the hudsons dull whitecaps
scarred from feathers of extinct birds
and lenape prayers
i turn toward the shadows of dead trees on the other
side of the tracks
waiting on the train in albany

it is winter
lights from the fuel truck glitter in the mud
the days are cold and nothing can dissuade
the slow malaise
of this city

someones car has stalled at the side of the road
through dry grass the emergency blinkers
are a swaying metaphor of loss

here are only the darkened faces
of trees
the tracks of their shadows

and the moon

nov 29/91–may 3/93

pastoral

a butterfly lands on the jagged edge of a broken
stained glass window
black flies spawn in winter grass

a wooden fence follows an upward slope into a stand
of sumac
disappears in the darkening folds of oak
and willow trees

suddenly the sun breaks through clouds
the colors of a van gogh landscape
and you are there
in the hues that twist and curve in beautiful despair

shadows lean upon one another
a windchime turns slowly on the porch
behind me
without sound . . .

new berlin ny
april 4 1990

a midland poem

it is dark
outside a calm wind circles
the hand print of dawn

the lamps and chairs are covered
with the dust of emptiness

a dog barks
a moth drags its body across the coffee table
sits undulating on a postcard of monets
poppy field
its ashen shadow disappears into a dark
stand of trees

suddenly it is afternoon
a pale house in the distance
a woman with an umbrella is walking
with a child in dry summer grass

they have grown forever alone

in a field of red flowers

5/31/90

untitled

a whirling wind of snow on a hill near
interstate 91 south
we drive the one open lane toward boston

crossing into new hampshire two crows
fly low over a river

there is the acrid smell of pollution in
a valley where birch and cedar
lean from the wind

later crossing the merrimac
classical music on the radio

the road is a dim vine branching in a thousand
directions across this land

i am a passenger grown tired of its promises
and its lies

2/12/88

lines from lima ohio for nan arbuckle

1
in the shadow of a silo a broken haywagon
at a farm near woodville

2
in a shadow that has awakened me beside this
motel bed
i watch the orange rag of dawn
limp like an old man across the room

3
something had divided me from the birds singing
and the moth down gathered where your fingers
touched the window

4
a starling calls among dark leaves
snowflakes tremble and disappear in the palm
of your hand
while you are dreaming
a light mist glitters in sunlight
on the window ledge

may 1990

lines for america

somehow i have never forgotten the motion
of sudden aloneness
when each moment that fixes us upon the earth
seems more alive

whether standing on the red earth of my homeland

or on a street in la
watching the dead air rise and fall
like the coal dust i watched from the bus window
at martins ferry ohio
covering everything like a suffering american dream

i stood watching while the
sun shadowed these things and gazed in terrible awe
not knowing what i was afraid of
not knowing that all around me
you were disappearing

12/28/87

journal entries march 12 & 13 1988
from greensboro bend vermont to little rock arkansas

i rest in the dark shallow i have found this morning
the coffee cup smoking in sunlight on the table
a warm light that seems so familiar
i look at the vermont landscape
its cold face in this morning light is still

in a small park in hartford massachusetts
there is a stone angel with outstretched wings and pigeon crap
on her head

awakening just after dawn we pass under low moving rainclouds in
tennessee
there is the vague light of spring in the clear darkness on the ridges
i miss the early crow songs i know are being sung here
i wish i could escape the whistling wind in these bus windows
in this early morning sunlight

one hundred miles out of knoxville
road construction has obliterated the other side of the interstate
for miles the red dirt rich with last nights rain glistens
in intermittent sunlight
americas machinery making roads for its new horses
there are ancestral horses underneath us warning us to be careful
with what is left
the dreaming horses echoing in the marrow of this land

there are these winter trees where birds nest
there is rain on the distant appalachians
the strange kindnesses of smiles and the passage of time
i have not spoken to anyone in six hundred miles
i am grateful to know what is left of me
to be calm in the center of that knowledge
and though i thought of you just now
there are passing clouds to watch
and high up
a hawk circling down the tattered pathway
to a mouse

last night riding into the darkness of america
i climbed comfortably toward sleep and paused there just at the edge
in a tenuous peace
there was a cheyenne song in my head and its singing found a way
through my voice
this day riding a long trail to little rock to read poems
i lean back feeling my real name and close my eyes to the
pure and collective dark that knows all our names

song for warriors
for bill dunnam

just west of watonga
after hours of beers at fats place

my friend stops the car
i walk to the carcass of badger
and cut one claw
from a front foot

lost in a blur of road and coors
i feel a deeper loss
in the scent
in the blessing on my hands

in the mountains above viarreggio

1
walking into cloud for a mile
the quiet settles to stillness and woodsmoke

2
just before dawn
i stand on an overlook listening
a screech owl lifts from a pine tree
and the world shudders

3
this afternoon is the sound of bells around the
necks of sheep
two birds i cannot recognize call to one another
down from this terrace a stone house glistens
in ancient clothes

4/24/89
6/26/89

27

take leave of the sun, and of the earth, for me
miguel hernandez spanish prisoner 1942

the moon places its handprint upon the earth
and against the skys vacuous dark
a whippoorwill

what the night harvests
is a wheat of fullness a wheat of voices
the chaff of human light

i place an empty cup on the table
in this room
i turn toward the direction of a sudden draft of wind

a winter wind outside pours over everything
while the moon sings

la sketch

1
nine am on the way to the ucla campus
we pass adobe walled motels
where the undocumented workers live

they line the streets begging for work
a dozen men argue with each other around a gray mercedes
two veho* inside laughing

under a santa monica throughway bridge
others are cooking breakfast on a hibachi
spanish music playing on their ghetto blaster

2
four o clock in the afternoon
somewhere near downtown
we pass the cheyenne liquor store
from the back seat wishing i had a drink
i turn and watch the sign blur and disappear
in the smog

3
three am
it is lorcas moon
heavy air tinged with ocean green

from the balcony of a small apartment
my hand brushes the misted railing

i lean back putting my feet up
opening the last beer before sleep

*cheyenne for white man and spider

untitled

this afternoon looking for my
grandmothers words
i remember a half eaten
pear browning on her window
sill
and her telling me the
stones i brought her
from europe were singing inside
her dreams

i see her folding the brightest
days of her life
into a small buckskin square

her sorrow colored days have become this gray
michigan sky

repose

nights wing crosses over us
the moon is gone

from the veranda i watch the old men
gathering at the bus stop

under graying clouds that have come
in from the sea
there is little to do but listen

to the gathering incongruities of darkness

someone is burning kelp at the edge of the estuary
smoke billows upward losing itself in the mist

across from the balcony where i stand
a widow is sorting socks

holding them to her in front of the mirror
while the wind touches her hair

riva trigoso italy
1/19/90

portraits from the blue note lounge
for danny "doc" white

in here starlight shines even on the shoes of the poor
darkness strolls from the trees across the street into the bar
crawls under the pool table and goes to sleep
moths gather and flutter under the streetlights
their wings grow heavy and damp

a candle flickers in the words of a song
the blues is a bow-necked guitar hanging on the wall
and a green plant under a busch beer sign
raindrops sliding down the window

a cat in the alley is thinking of seafood
the guys at the v.a. dream horrid dreams
always incoming

a city bus whines past
some lost soul uncovers from a tarp blinking
into the red tail lights

on 23rd street a hooker just escaped from a
whore house in houston
smiles
fingering an empty juicy fruit gum wrapper
in her pocket

i reach past these blurred images toward a bottle
of bud and remember
the blues reminds us that all journeys begin
by leaving
and by closing time
    we'll all be gone

late summer

voice on looking glass in an unlit house
the floor an odor of sky

it is morning
caught in wan light
soliloquy of someone who has lost the wind

we carry inside this flame of dark clove
a thing cared for
that has never spoken

color of thread where the season departs
wing of cloud

these are the small husks in dreamt water
moving toward us where we wake
late in the afternoon
wrapped in leaves pale and alone

10/2/85

lines from a revolutionary text II

i have seen you
gathering the tiniest things

so they could not be taken
from your hands

11/28/93

night arrives dressed in the memory of itself
in the fresh and luminous
edges of its wind
i hear leaves that ring as an ocean
while gray clouds stain the moon
dreams the color of ashes
fly past the window

here in this
late hour
a lone dog is weeping for its master

telluride co
1/3/94

dream of birds
for roberta hill whiteman

1
dawn rises
things appear from a horizon of crows
fragments of recognition as if in dream

where the hand remembers reaching
where you tremble near the shattered edge of words

dusk is an arc of drifting heron

2
a warm wind turns north
a woman falls into the heart of a flower
this is an hour standing apart

open as a door or a hawk whose shadow
is a circling night

for tom krampf

in western new york near olean
it is snowing in the yard of my friend
he will waken to the long hill outside his window
turned white as sea foam

at noon he will look back over his words

the french clock will grind into a new hour
and he will listen
again
to the ashes growing dark in the cold wood stove
and the onions in the hanging net
growing bright with sunlight
in another room

riva trigoso italy
1/4/89

untitled
for george trakl

a bird sits on a branch for a long time
the bee in a flower lifts its voice in praise
each moment is a small life
remembering

and lost suddenly in transparencies
i wait in a wind that has blown
my name away
in a vacuous room i watch
a candle flame
its wavering shadow light
on the walls
in the song of an abandoned bird
in the dark sounds of night that
settle like mist
on our sleeping

your voice is a lengthening whisper
in the rain
i have come again
alone and without answers . . .

wandering the rubble of dreams
the illusions of days
and voices and winds

i wander daily past faces merged
into a tapestry of stars

just after noon
va alcohol recovery ward oklahoma city

this day two other indians were brought
in from the county jail
gaunt and without light thcy walk
unsteadily down the hall

i envision a photograph of 1869
three captive cheyennes wrapped in army
blankets standing near horses at camp supply oklahoma

wordless and lost in this america that has destroyed so many

i think of ortiz*
and gogisgi*

and ask a blessing for their way

we are the true veterans of this land

*simon ortiz, native american poet and veteran
*cherokee name of carroll arnett, poet and veteran

untitled

under the earths misted arc
a field of sage lit by the fire
of night
bursts through the curtains

i waken to sit in the dark fragrance lit
by the moon
hours crystallize
into strands of winds

i look to the room where my grandmother
slept
the corner where she sat and smoked

spirals of smoke echo now
soft petals of solitude

finished with light

6/18/83
8/7/89

journal entry on a greyhound bus
for maurice kenny

dusk the sound of a woman softly singing
the suns warm and waning light empties the trees of their
long shadows that spill to the ground
leaving memphis
under a bridge someones tarp flaps like a thing torn from
a dream
it is sunday evening
the miwok kid in front of me takes a long pull
on a whiskey bottle
i watch the steady drone of headlights
the gray road whining beneath me
hours from tomorrow
the dark trees are slow men in weary coats
watching us pass . . .

columbus day* october 12 1988
for jeanetta

driving east toward columbus ohio
storm clouds the same gray as this american interstate

we pass stubble fields of corn
and leaves bright with autumnal color

later sitting at a kentucky fried chicken shop
a mayflower truck drifts by

i remember that in websters dictionary the word
genoa is just above genocide

america is a name
we indians wear sunglasses to escape

america is a dead autumn leaf
fallen to ground

*a protest poem in conjunction with the international day of
solidarity with american indians suggested by the yanonami indians
of brazil at the united nations in geneva switzerland august 1988

veterans hospital
oklahoma city oklahoma for my brothers

at 2 am someone is walking down
a long hallway
the color of fatigue in his thousand
yard eyes

i want to call to him
telling him that i forgive him

i want him to tell me
that he forgives me

2/9/88

43

this is no arizona highways poem

mid afternoon
driving through globe
my sister drunk in the back seat naming all
the bars the skins hang out in

after passing the san carlos apache
reservation
i watch shaky dreams made of rain
in the rear view mirror

pulling into a station for gas
the wipers create a surreal picture
of this city

my mouth cotton dry after driving non stop
from oklahoma

were just indians lost in the blur
of america

and again

we have come to bury our dead

10/27/87

leaving bents fort
for floyd bringing good

riding the high plains from colorado
to kansas
a whirlwind gaunt and alone crosses the landscape

i drive the truck south toward oklahoma
crossing the same path two moon and roman nose
once wandered

i am on the edge

barely in america

somewhere between rage and freedom

45

oklahoma twilights

I
near wewoka in the first storm i have witnessed since
returning from the east coast

i watch to the north dark thunderclouds steeped
in furrows of wind

a long hungered autumn loosens its clouds upon the earth

plagued by a winterful of whispers
i feel my life watching me

from a swaying treeline . . .

march 29 88

II
riding into the endless plains
the night filled with questions asks me the things
i have endured

without answers i roll the window partially down
smell the early clove of dark whistling past

caught in the weariness of another oklahoma
sundown i turn to jeanetta asking her where we are
ask her to accompany me across this stretch
of darkness
to a place near dawn
a place we can limp
to pray

III
for jeanetta

near the arkansas river across from tulsa
a delaware woman climbs small boulders to sit
near a ragged tree

among silver spider webs
she sits in somber unsoundable prayer

after a long while she raises her arms toward
the river

no one can know this small moment and its beautiful
sadness better than her

IV
for michael west

i watch down a road of white dust
and hear the slow voices under the earth
wandering in the scattered message of a dark
farewell

my brother is walking past empty villages
where innocence resided
past stone walls and jars wracked by the words
of children abandoned

my eyes and heart were born into this terrifying beauty
its strangeness a cloth of slow dusk
the sun a prayer wafer floating in water

where is the promise that once filled this land
i asked this question once and since
have learned to become alone and angry
and hidden

on the borderlines of america

sitting outside in early morning

a single face follows me out of sleep
summers wind through chimes at morning

a white crane lands beyond my sight
near waters edge

having watched a long time
i withdraw under the sound of locusts

a breeze settles like ash
on everything

day breaks open this way

travelling from new york to vermont
for maurice kenny

crossing on the grand isle ferry
at plattsburg
shards of ice crunch underneath

a blacktail hawk perched on a bare limb
breaks the monotony
of the winter skyline

its body a study of solemn beauty

etched in silence
and white

lines begun at mahopac lake

snow falling on ches hands
the hollow eyes filling with the skys lament
sitting here by a lake filled with winter sunlight
the small buds of an acacia bush are weeping and cold

a turtle crawls by outside the window
names from the nam memorial on its back

its new years eve
the flowers on the table are in vases made
of memory

dark trees silhouetted against a napalm dusk
the train stops at poughkeepsie
an empty bird nest fills with early starlight

across the aisle a child folds into dream
a low mist gathers on the hudson

three days after wounded knee 1890 the bodies of lakota
women and children freezing and alone
were brought into the fort
this place where crazy horse was assassinated

a sign above the post gate read
peace on earth goodwill to men

two fragments april 10/92

a murmur of geese
follows the angling river north
clothed in a dream
their wings sore with dusk

north country rain
a birds hushed song caught in a droplet on a tree branch
no thunder
i sit in lamp light
an occasional car whines by outside
this is the time lorca named duende
an hour made of essential things
flowers in lightless water
a horse wandering aimlessly toward a village with no name

guilderland ny
march 1992

lines and texts 3/21/92

the clear sky of long island filled with stars
their frozen wings are silent

the cup in the wooden cupboard trembles

filled with gray winter light

ohio sketches

1
dawn light
brushes the window pane
a low hovering mist descends upon the corn fields
a dog's distant bark

2
rain drops on the window
the road shines into the sky
an endless metaphor the silos reflect
in their dreaming pastures
a crow feather makes its way down a rivulet into a drainage ditch

3
how many windows will loneliness look into tonight
flecked with rain or snow or the ringing solace of fingerprints .
reaching out toward something remembered
something bright

west liberty ohio
1/3/92

from calumet

two days out of oklahoma
i recall the orange panorama
of sunset
over twelve mile point

soft dressers* headstone leaning into
timelessness

ours is a landscape turned inward
our words escaping whispers under swirling stars

tsistsistas*
i have thrown my name into the water

a full moon shimmering on the surface

*a relative who died at age 18—in 1886—buried in my familys
cemetery near twelve mile point calumet oklahoma
*the name we cheyenne call ourselves

a remembrance
after reading at an opening of curtis photographs

writing in this half light
there is the hushed breathing of sleep
a shadow of leaves moving behind the curtain

in fragmented dream you turn
your eyes in sleep as you will tell me later
searching the landscape of your grandmothers
hands

what did little wolf see
the cold dawn over fort robinson
his shadow yearning for flight in the
passing shadows of geese

dull knifes people
leaning from their hiding places
the metallic taste of fear in their breath
bitten by frost and sorrow

a soft winter rain begins
i watch in silence
the rivulets on the winter glass
lit by streetlights

park hotel den haag
the netherlands
10/22/92

55

ohio landscape

nothing changes the pictures on the walls
an occasional bird passing by the windows
the wind that settles upon the dimmed lamps does not boast
of its journey for the sea

so it goes here
except for an almost incomprehensible smile
crossing your lips as you sleep

the leaves have lost their hold upon the sky
someone is listening to a song from long ago

1/29/92

untitled

1
just under this balcony
a small garden in bird song
and shadow
a leaf falls like a lost prayer
into the water
howling wolfs drawings
stare out from the yellowing pages
of a book
drawn with the ease of quiet persistence
a warriors persistence
hou . . .
look at mother earth
she is watching you sing

2
the birds of morning grow dark
as their shadows
a man holds an umbrella over
the head of a young girl
laughter reaches out from the
pictures wrapped in the gentle
otter braids of dreams

a slow singing of beads begins
on a blanket
disappearing into a message that is
timeless
and resembles the wintered breath
of sand creek

what ever you wanted to say
what ever you laughed or
wept for
is here in this very moment
in this silence

edith swans house
oberlin oh
10/2/92

desert sketches
10/9/92

three weeks ago in gallup
at the red light on central

i watched down the street the neon lights
of bars

barely noon

and the staggering has already begun

last night at zuni
i walked past the school into a field
toward high buttes below the moon

later i watched the milky way grow
out of the darkness

already the leaves of autumn were there

a dogs bark disappearing in high desert
wind

at the navajo school
a whirlwind of red dust made its way
slowly across the road

in half dream i saw my shadow running
back toward me
my face felt a warmth like a wind
or a breath

i wanted to say to you
of all the shadows i have ever seen
the one made by humans is the most alone

at rock point
my son kneels beside desert sage
and the track of a horse

his shadow becomes the roundness
of a prayer

he looks across the desert
wordless in the silence
of a million years

the wind is touching his hair

high back wolf*

wrapped in a muted presence
your voice stilled from the wind
of summit springs
the light from a thousand moons
colors your brow

you stare out from wounds that have
marked forever your enemies
who now wish to be like you
in white sweat lodges and crystal
hallucinations
their god forever damned

see how your sacrifice is a prayer
the red tail flies

now the silent bell of recognition
dances before you

maheo shivadom

soon my brother

you will come home

*a cheyenne chief who was killed at the summit springs
fight in 1868; his body was not found until two years
ago when it was discovered taxidermied . . . standing in a
museum in lansing nebraska

for bob cook*

eastern ohio at three am
the streetlamp is a bone tinted light
the woods behind this house are lost
in darkness

all day i have followed the years back
toward my grandfather
his smile at a passing bird

his memory a cloud
turning a thousand images in my dreams

somewhere ohkom*
crosses under a fence he built

moonlight glistening
on its

graying

back

*priest, native american church, chapter #1 calumet ok &
henson's grandfather
*cheyenne for coyote

lines for a yuki* brother

among the notes on a morning train
the song is darkness and passing lights

oandason told me he was going north
to visit and settle himself

all day these netherlands clouds have
threatened rain

i remember the balcony in la where
we passed a bottle of wine

and the ocean mist

ultrecht netherlands
10/5/92

*a tribe nearly exterminated by the racists of california
wm oandason held on until the fall of 1992

lines near calumet

moments and days i had forgotten

a broken wing on a cedar bough
the coffee half finished on the table

across the wavering heat line
of an abandoned field

i reach toward you who have been
gone for so long

and pull back the torn
garment
of a prayer

for the blalocks
july 1/93–nov 7/93

songhla province

the road from hatyai airport
lined with bamboo leafed
restaurants
dark faces in smiles and poverty

potholes and rusted signs
like the road from calumet to concho*

it is indian country here

guerrillas from maylasia have crossed
the border
burned schools and fired upon trains

i stare out from the bus window

red earth

a water buffalo
grazing at the edge of a rice paddy

thailand
9/20/93

*indian road in cheyenne country oklahoma

maybe the invaders are wearing out

just inside the oklahoma border
at the side of the
interstate
in tall weeds
an abandoned trailer
the windows shot out

a 78 ford pickup that hasnt run
for years
sitting by the door

12/22/93–1/3/94

a new poem for elisabetta

as sudden as blue frost
after awakening

someone turns

the sorrowed signal of lateness
on everything

we seem so estranged
from the cup of courage
of laughter

darkness and the yellow moon

i will look for you somewhere in the
marrow of the sea

riva*
i cannot forget

is this how far i have travelled
from you

on a plane from ny to milano
5/11/93–11/7/93

*riva trigosa, a small town in liguria italy

66

catching the bus in lee mass
for peter, lynn & sarah kinne

the ashen sky in a soliloquy of wind
gathers toward rain
no bird song here
only the silent passage of afternoon

a man stares out from the pharmacy
where i bought my ticket
i stare back
waiting for his interest to wane
and he looks away

in a light rain
i close my eyes to the memory
of sweat rocks singing
and the sacred fire i kept all day the day before

outside this bus window
a hazed dimness
weaves its way along the road

as i look west

toward home

6/6/93–6/30/93

67

a woman in winter

i know you are remembering
as the year that seemingly just began
slides from the calendar into the void

the room where outside a bird was singing
in an unkempt garden you could not see
until you opened the curtain

a light snow in the cornfields

telluride co
12/30/93

four pieces
for danyelle miletic*

we stared out the train window
our faces brushing the night landscape that passed
in its hurried way beyond the glass

five months ago
somewhere in italy
your notebook a shimmering voice of passion
its torn and ragged pages in your own words
whispering as only the hunted can whisper

it is the darks own leaping
out of our mouths
from under our shoes
in the pieces of light in a dense forest
surrounding our lives . . . and we learn to say
goodbye to the things we love

we can hear sleep
drawing its water from the smallest breath
the wind standing at the edge of a myth
in its wounds there is also the scar of a smile
that has darkened

it is still winter in your voice
she said
i lit a cigar and watched a worlds sadness drifting in her eyes

in america at the edge of a freeway a man is holding a torn cup
filled with darkness
it is a kind of darkness i have seen before

albuquerque nm
3/12/93

*a bosnian young woman i met on a train in italy. she was fleeing the
war in sarajevo

february 25 1994
a birthday poem from vienna austria for jeanetta

waiting on a train
i remember the danube in mist

and near the hungarian border
just yesterday
i slept and saw you
a changeling caught in the light
of the morning star
your smile the guesting birds in flight

a small wet leaf
pressed its face against the car window

i remained just as i was
as i am now

sitting in a murmurous wind

regent hotel

what is this shadow play
dark silhouettes that move against each other
upon a bordered wall

on CNN a child without a face
moves from side to side
in a crib in sarajevo

outside this window
two dragons atop a pagoda

are fighting over the moon

singapore
9/16/93–11/27/93

for bukowski
on hearing of his death

here in paris
a small kitten purrs at the waning moon

you are gone
far from the blessed nights
where you vomited the terrorous
joy of your life

this dutch army coat smells of
cigar smoke and the yellow
clouds of a dangerous sky

a man looks a long time
at the rain

some of it falls into his beer

march 20 1994

lines from a revolutionary text III

the veho world is crumbling
nothing made from ignorance

will remain

mahago do miutz
ehi woh